HOW MONEY WORKS

YOUR MONEY

By Gerry Bailey
and Felicia Law
Illustrated by Mark Beech

(checker border) ©Eskemar/Shutterstock; 17 ©Denizo71/Shutterstock; 17–18 ©JNP/Shutterstock; 25 (l) ©JCVStock/Shutterstock; 25 (r) ©Sarah2/Shutterstock; 35 (t) ©JNP/Shutterstock; 35 (c) ©ESB Professional/Shutterstock; 35 (b) © Shutterstock; 36 ©Kateryna Tsygankova/Shutterstock; 41 ©Huguette Roe/Shutterstock; 42 ©sirtravelalot/Shutterstock; 44 (t) ©3777190317/Shutterstock; 44 (b) ©Northfoto/Shutterstock; 47 ©Andrey N. Bannov/Shutterstock; 54 ©Hung Chung Chih/Shutterstock

Houghton Mifflin Harcourt Edition

Printed in the U.S.A.

ISBN 978-1-328-52370-9

5 6 7 8 9 10 11 12 0607 29 28 27 26 25 24 23 22 21

4500843224 A B C D E F G

HOW MONEY WORKS

YOUR MONEY

HOW YOU SPEND YOUR MONEY – AND WHY

HMH

Contents

Words that appear in red throughout the text are defined in the glossary on pages 62–63.

What is Money?

The obvious answer to this question is that money is the stuff jingling in your pocket or purse, as well as the bills that seem to vanish as quickly as you get them. Money is used to buy things.

But is it still money if it is a debit card or credit card? A note from a foreign country? Electronic money?

MONEY PROMISES

Money is basically a promise that it can be used and has value. So that would cover coins and bills in your country's currency, electronic money, debit and credit cards, and foreign currencies. They are all forms of paying for things, which is what money can do. Some forms are easier to access than others. The easiest being coins and bills in your country's currency.

MONEY MOVES

It doesn't take much to see that money is still changing its shape and form. Also, money isn't being used in the same way everywhere. This is mainly because money isn't just about currency – coins and notes, or even credit cards. It's about banks and savings, and money that flows around the world.

THE HISTORY OF MONEY

As we find out just what is and what isn't seen as money today, we'll discover that all sorts of crazy forms of money have cropped up in the past – amber, beads, cowrie shells, drums, eggs, and feathers, to name just a few.

In fact, you could use anything as money – even a few sheep – as long as everyone agreed on their value.

Money has been around in one form or another for thousands of years! The fact is that money wasn't just invented in one place. It developed in all kinds of ways and in many different parts of the world.

But no matter what object was used as money, it always had 4 qualities:

* Everyone agreed to use it.
* Everyone agreed that it could be used in different ways.
* Everyone agreed that it had a value which might change but which everyone would accept.
* Everyone agreed to respect what it stood for.

SO LET'S FIND OUT HOW MONEY WORKS FOR YOU.

Money Is a “Must”

Do you have money? Do you have money jingling in your pocket today? A wallet full of coins and bills? Or a piggy bank where you put all those spare coins? Even a savings or bank account of your own?

YOU HAVE MONEY!

If you have any of these, you have money! And it's likely that you'll have more and more money as the months and years go by.

IN AND OUT

Money is like water – it flows freely – in and out of everyone's pockets. It will definitely flow in and out of your pocket for most of your life, but will it flow out faster than it flows in?

If it flows in, you're earning. You may have to work for the money, or you may be given it as pocket money, a gift, or a scholarship fund. If it flows out, you're spending. You're buying things and paying for them. If it flows in faster than it flows out, you'll be fine. If it doesn't, you'll have problems.

MONEY'S FUN, TOO!

Earning it is fun and spending it is definitely fun!

But you can do something even better! You can "grow" your money by saving it with interest in a bank. When you are older you can also invest it. Investing means giving the money to financial people that will use it in order to make more money. Now that can be a real challenge and fun! Sometimes you make money, but sometimes you lose money when you invest.

You can also share your money. You can share it with people who will be helped in a really big way. Imagine being able to help someone like that!

SOME THINGS ABOUT MONEY ...

* We think about it and talk about it.
* We love having it and couldn't buy things without it.
* We need it for necessities like food and shelter.
* We enjoy it for the fun things it buys.

So money is a "must." It's something you can't escape from, but that doesn't have to be a bad thing. Just the opposite – it's something you can take control of, have fun with, grow, spend, and help people with.

Money Goes Around

SPENDING PUTS YOUR MONEY INTO CIRCULATION

You pass money across a counter for goods. The cashier passes it to the bank who passes it to people – and so on, and so on.

1

You buy a pack of gum and put your coins on the counter.

2

The coins find themselves in and out of another four cash registers that same day.

3 This happens again and again.

6 The change falls into a child's hand. In half an hour, it's being handed over the counter to the cashier of the local candy store.

5

The bank holds them just two days before they're delivered to the owner of an amusement arcade to be given out as change.

4

Over the weekend, they're bagged and delivered to the bank.

Becoming part of the Money Cycle

* The role of young people in moving money around is growing, and this involves YOU.

* You're not just a buyer, a consumer, you're already an important part of the money cycle.

* Young people have never had so much money, and spending isn't the only thing you can do with it! It's time for you to get started on money management.

* Jobs for young people are changing. Past generations often held jobs "for life." Young people will change jobs more often; this can lead to earning more money if you are creative and flexible.

The future is all before you. You are probably more money-wise than your parents were at your age – and the opportunities before you can be far greater.

Receiving Money

It's always great when you're surprised with a gift of money. You might get a small thrill from finding a coin on the sidewalk or from stumbling across a shoebox of cash in the trash. Odds are that both these things won't come your way! But (surprise! surprise!) there might be a stash of cash with your name on it right now, or coming your way sometime in the future, that might change your life.

BIRTHDAY MONEY

You may have been given money for your birthday by your favorite relatives – perhaps you even received money when you were born, in which case a parent may have already opened a bank or savings account in your name. Could they have been putting money away into an account for years and have forgotten to tell you about it?

TRUST MONEY

Parents can establish a trust fund for you. Sometimes adults set up trust funds at a bank, or put money in a savings account where it's invested until such time as a child is old enough to have access to it for themselves. Usually, an age is established before which the funds cannot be touched.

INHERITING MONEY

A sad way to get money is to inherit it when a person dies. A will is a legal document that says how a person's assets will be handed down after their death. If no will exists, a dead person is said to be intestate and laws have to be used to decide the list of heirs. You might still inherit, but a stranger might decide just what you get!

YOUR ASSETS

It goes without saying that if any of these situations drop into your lap, they should be used wisely. If you have money in savings bonds, or trust funds, or bank accounts, or anything else, you have what's called assets. Assets establish your financial value, known as your net worth. The older you get, the more important your net worth will be. It may allow you to get a loan to buy your dream purchase, to help you through college, or to fund that student trip.

ALLOWANCE MONEY

A REGULAR INCOME

Allowance money is your first step to receiving a regular income. It can be relied on to come in each week, more or less on time, and in full. You can "bank on it" as they say, which also means you can be planning how you're going to spend it long before it arrives.

You may receive a weekly or monthly allowance depending on how the family budget is arranged. It will also depend on how far you can be trusted to stick to a financial plan, known as a budget.

ARE YOU GETTING AN ALLOWANCE?

There are different opinions about the value of giving allowances or pocket money to young people, and you may find parents need a little persuasion. You may have parents who already know all of this – they believe it's important for you to start handling your own money at a young age.

HOW MUCH?

How much pocket money you get depends on how much money your family has available to give you or how much they think you should have.

Bearing in mind that parents want the best for you, accept pocket money as you would accept a gift. After all, that's what it really is. Even if it's a small amount, it's worth establishing that you're grateful.

Memo to parents

* Having pocket money is good for your child.
* It encourages a sense of independence.
* It helps kids understand the value of money.
* It teaches them to make decisions on whether to spend it all right away, or save for a few weeks so they can buy something special.

Ages and stages

Increase pocket money by a fixed amount on each birthday. If your child is old enough to help out with household chores, arrange increases in pocket money in exchange for more involvement around the house.

THOSE CHORES!

You may get a weekly allowance in return for taking responsibility for certain chores around the house. It's unlikely you'll grow up in a world where wads of cash continue to come your way free of responsibilities, so this is good practice for the future.

STRINGS ATTACHED!

So – with pocket money comes responsibility. If pocket money has strings attached that require you to carry out certain chores, it's worth making an agreement, or a contract, with whoever is paying, which details EXACTLY what they expect of you.

SMALL JOBS MAKE A DIFFERENCE

Chores may be simply helping around the kitchen or involve just keeping your own room clean – which you should be doing anyway! They may involve caring for pets, washing the car, or work in the yard.

These chores help your parents out and involve you in taking on some of the workload of the entire household.

IT'S IN THE CONTRACT

Why is it important to have this "contract" decided up front? Once you've agreed what you get paid for and what you don't, parents will expect you to stick to this. Expect trouble when you don't live up to expectations – if you forget to make your bed, turn off the lights downstairs, or if you leave the dog outside.

A few useful chores can cement the pocket money contract at home.

DO IT ANYWAY!

There are, of course, parents who think that helping with the household chores should be part of your involvement anyway and don't think they should have to pay you for this.

Jobs you can do

* Garage cleaner
* Painter of garden furniture/fences
* Gardener
* Car washer
* Snow shoveler
* Window cleaner
* Horse helper
* Plant sitter
* Deliveries
* Party entertainer: clown, magician, balloon artist, storyteller, actor, musician
* Animals' shelter worker: clean kennels, walk dogs, feed animals
* Pet sitter
* Adopt a grandma/grandpa
* Computer design: making cards, signs, etc.
* Plant sales: grow herbs in small pots
* Sell old clothes, toys, games
* T-shirt design

EARNING MONEY

It isn't long before you begin to understand that the most reliable way of getting money is to earn it. Your pocket money or allowance may already come with strings attached – the odd household chore for a buck or two. But joining the labor market – selling your time, effort, and expertise outside the home – not only brings in the cash, but can give you a lot more benefits as well.

FIRST JOB

Your first job will probably be in addition to your schoolwork. Don't underestimate the demands. If you take on work, you will need to be committed to it for the time it takes. Work will need to be a priority just like school is.

Added to this, you won't want to give up your sports activities or your social or family life. So fitting it all in will take extra doses of energy and organization. Make sure you've thought this all out before you take the leap.

Regular work can be taken on to earn extra allowance.

REWARD FOR EFFORT

Finally, you'll be earning money that rewards your effort and contribution – that should make you feel good! You should get a real sense of personal accomplishment and a confidence boost!

Lots of power. Use it wisely!

Young people exercise enormous control over family spending through "pester power," the power to persuade parents to spend money. More than two-thirds of teens say they have the power to influence their parents' buying decisions. And they twist them around their little fingers ...

Researchers have repeatedly found that parents hate saying "no" to teens. They're more likely to go without something themselves than deny their children.

Three Choices

Money is just a piece of metal or paper – or a plastic card – until you use it to make something happen. You can use it in just 3 different ways – you either spend it, save it, or give it away. Any one of these will bring different results.

SPEND IT!

For those who like to spend, money is the best thing that ever happened. It's the key to hours of shopping and owning things – new things. It can be the trigger to a bad habit – to shop for shopping's sake!

It can also be the entry to new experiences and adventures, helping you to join clubs and make contacts who share your interests. If you have spent your money wisely, then you have the benefit of all those new possessions or experiences.

SAVE IT!

It's amazing how some people can save money easily. It seems to come naturally to them. People can be as different about the way they handle money as they are in the way they look, or the things they're interested in.

You save money by simply not spending the money you earn or are given. If it's just a few coins, you can save it in a piggy bank. But when you get more, you may want to put it in a bank that will give you a little extra, called interest, each month.

GIVE IT AWAY!

Sharing is something you usually do because you want to, not because you have to. Handouts to friends are probably done knowing your friends will return the favor sometime. But it feels good to actually help someone who desperately needs it. There are plenty of people in this situation. Dropping a few coins into a charity box each week means that someone somewhere will be helped by YOU. And you could get directly involved and actually see how your contribution is helping.

Save It!

SLEEPING CASH

If, to you, saving means stashing all your cash in your mattress and letting it lie there, then you will find that what you can buy with your stash will decrease. And if you pop it into your piggy bank, then it will sit there doing nothing, with the same results. So this is not the kind of saving you want to be doing.

WORKING CASH

Instead, there are ways of saving, which, just like spending, involve putting your money into circulation. When you put your money into a savings account at the bank, you are trusting someone else to make it grow. It will be used to invest in businesses and earn a profit. And you get a share of that, even though it may be a small share, in the form of interest.

What kind of saver are you?

The NON-saver

- You spend without thinking about what you need or what you want.
- You buy all the newest luxuries and save nothing.
- Your money often runs out before more comes in.

The small saver

- You spend, but you think about what you need and what you want.
- Maybe you do without a luxury so you can save a bit.
- The money you save begins to add up.
- The more you have, the better you feel about it.
- You can still buy a few things when you want to.
- You can deal with emergencies.
- You can buy things that you couldn't afford with just a week's, or a month's, pocket money.
- You're learning life skills.

The BIG saver

- You spend as little as possible.
- You'd rather save money, so you spend only on necessities.
- You put as much as you can into the bank.

PIGGY BANKS

Most kids have owned a piggy bank at some time or another. But why a piggy bank? Why not a rhinoceros bank or an aardvark bank? Are pigs thought to be better than other animals at saving their hard-earned cash? Well – maybe, but that's not why we have piggy banks.

FATTENING UP!

In earlier times in Western societies, a pig was a kind of poor man's money box. A piglet, bought from the market in spring, could live on household leftovers and would be fattened up and ready for the butcher just before the winter. Your piggy bank, which is fed on leftovers of your money, fattens in the same way, and can be smashed to pieces when it's full.

In German-speaking countries, it was the custom to give apprentices – young people who were training to become craftsmen – a pig as reward for a year's work. The pig, therefore, became the symbol of investing – both with money and in young people!

PYGGS

Many years ago, people kept pots and jugs in their kitchen made from a kind of clay called pygg. When they wanted to put some money away, they'd put it in these pots or jars for safety. In time, the receptacles became known as pygg banks, then pyggy banks.

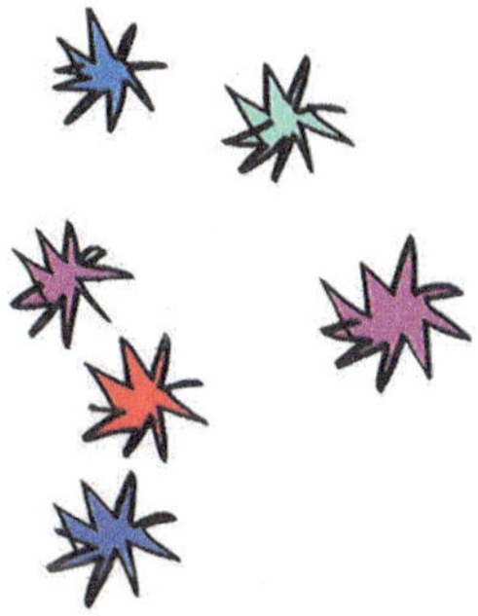

No doubt it didn't take long for someone to come up with the idea of a pygg bank actually shaped like a pig. And so the piggy bank was born.

Traditional clay pyggs looked like this.

The piggy bank we know today.

MONEY IN THE BANK

So you have some money and you've decided against the piggy bank and the mattress. But is it enough money to open a bank account? A bank will normally expect you to keep a minimum amount of money in your new account, enough to make it worth their while. If you dip below this amount, you may get charged a fee, so this is the first thing to find out.

WHAT'S IN IT FOR YOU?

The bank may require a minimum deposit. In exchange you get:

* somewhere to place your cash.
* a savings account with interest paid on the balance. (See page 29 to find out about calculating interest.)
* a debit card so you can withdraw cash from the ATM (Automated Teller Machine) and pay by card in stores.

OLD ENOUGH?

The BIG issue is age. If you want a bank account of your own, you will have to be 18 years old, or of legal age in many countries. But don't give up. Parents can help get an account opened. This doesn't mean that it belongs to them – you will still get privacy and your mail will be sent to you.

Bank accounts

Your bank will probably be able to set you up with Internet access to your account so you can find out at any time what is happening to your balance. There are two types of accounts.

Checking account

All banks will offer you a checking account – one that allows you to place, or deposit, money and withdraw it whenever you like. You won't get any interest on this because the amount may go up and down on the hour. However, some banks do pay interest on checking accounts if the balance hits a certain level – so it's best to ask. You should arrange to have a statement sent to you each month or you can check it online.

Savings account

To make sure that you are "growing" your money, you need to set up a savings account. There are various kinds that banks offer, dependent upon how much money you want to place and for how long. Obviously, the longer the bank can be certain that it has your cash, the better the deal it will offer you.

GROWING MONEY

One of the great things about money is that it doesn't lose value in itself. If you hide $5 under the mattress, you'll still have $5 when you go to find it later. It may not buy you as much, but it'll still be $5.

When you spend money on goods, things change. Goods depreciate. What does "depreciate" mean? It means that over time, the value you paid for something starts to decrease. The older most things get, the less they are worth if you wanted to sell them.

In some ways, money and goods behave in the same way. The goods get older and are worth less. The money stays the same, but the world outside changes. Rising prices make your money buy less – so it's worth less.

The only way to combat all this is to make your money grow.

Earning interest

When you put your money in your savings account at the bank, you expect your money to grow. This happens because the bank uses your money in its business investments and it will pay you a fee for this use. The fee is known as interest.

Interest is the profit or reward paid to the lender. Interest is interesting because anyone can do it and make their money grow a little – or sometimes a lot.

You can earn interest either as simple interest or compound interest.

Simple interest just keeps adding interest to your original amount. This is how it grows if your $1 earns interest at 10% for 5 years:

Simple Interest			
Year	Investment	Annual Rate	Ending Value
1	$1	10%	$1.10
2	$1	10%	$1.20
3	$1	10%	$1.30
4	$1	10%	$1.40
5	$1	10%	$1.50

Compound interest pays better than simple interest. The interest rate may be the same, and the time the same, but now the interest is added to the total savings AND the interest it has earned. It grows your money much faster.

Compound Interest			
Year	Investment	Annual Rate	Ending Value
1	$1	10%	$1.10
2	$1.10	10%	$1.21
3	$1.21	10%	$1.33
4	$1.33	10%	$1.46
5	$1.40	10%	$1.61

Spend it!

We all love spending money. It gives us the things we want, it makes us feel good – and it's not that difficult! There's no shortage of things to spend your money on. But just in case you run out of ideas, you're bombarded with ads on the street, in magazines, on TV, and – when you've actually bought something – even on your shopping bags.

WISE SPENDING

Spending money brings a certain responsibility. You can only spend the money you have. If you're careful with your spending, everything's fine. If you're reckless, you can end up in trouble.

THE VALUE OF MONEY

When adults lecture you about understanding the value of money, it's really this that they're talking about – knowing how to spend wisely.

What kind of SPENDER are you?

The NON-spender

* You keep every penny that comes your way.
* You do without – or "make do" – rather than use your precious cash to buy things.
* The money you don't spend begins to add up.

The CAREFUL spender

* You spend, but you think about what you need and what you want.
* Maybe you do without a luxury so you can save a bit.
* The money you save begins to add up.

The BIG spender

* You spend and spend and blow all your money.
* You feel good, you look good, you've got loads of stuff.
* You look "big" and successful to your friends.
* You've got "power in your pocket" – for the moment.
* When it's all gone, you come down with a bang.
* You never have anything put aside for emergencies.
* You never have enough for the fantastic thing you've always wanted but just can't afford.
* You overstretch your spending and sometimes have to borrow.

STORES

Most spending takes place in stores. Today, they are often modern, glitzy places full of excitement and appealing goods. But this is a fairly new development.

STORES DEVELOP

Stores have come a long way since the earliest days when peddlers used to walk the streets of cities and country roads, selling their goods from a small horse and cart or even from a simple tray.

And even when stores started to open on the main street, they would be pretty limited – a butcher, a baker, and a candlestick maker, to name a few.

Your grandparents, maybe their parents, will remember a time when there were few clothing stores, no music stores, and certainly no electronics stores selling computers and TVs.

STOCK IT!

Do you expect to buy goldfish food at the grocery store? A hair comb in the paper store? A newspaper at the garage? Many stores specialize their stock to sell only certain types of items.

Stores can also sell a range of products. Some stores can carry everything a community might need and other stores, like convenience stores, carry a limited selection to keep things simple and easy.

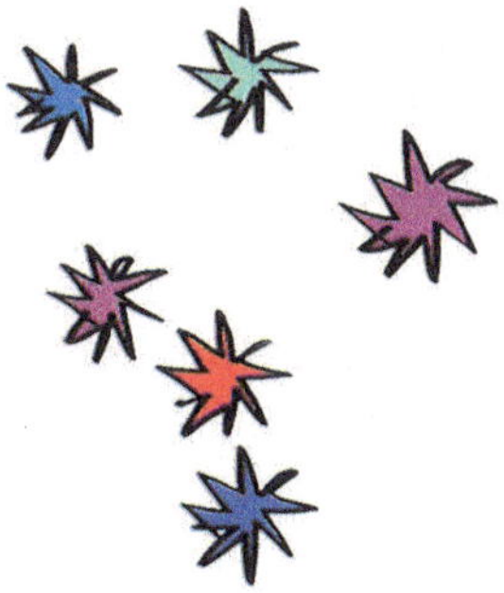

PRICE

Price is important. People have a limited amount of money to spend, and if they spend more on one thing, they cannot spend it on another.

Generally when the price of a product goes up, other competitive and cheaper products will sell better. People buy more hamburger if the price is $1.00 per pound than if it is $2.00 per pound.

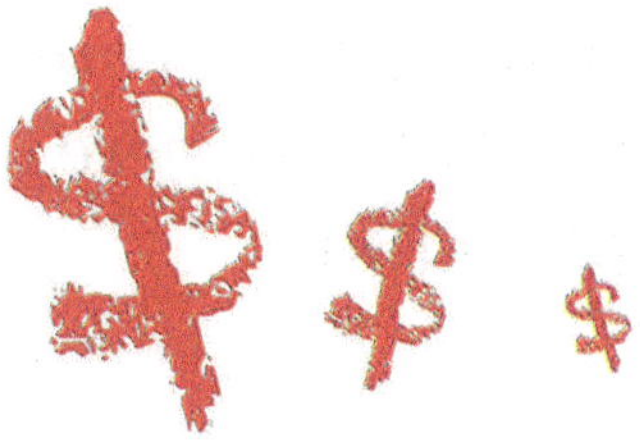

GOING SHOPPING

Which are your favorite stores? You'll certainly have some. One of the most surprising things about our shopping habits is that we tend to visit a few favorite stores over and over again and rarely change our shopping pattern. We like the way the stores are laid out, the goods they carry, or the people that work there!

We like the fact that when we visit them, everything is exactly as we would expect to find it. There are no surprises. We feel comfortable. And the store planners know this, so they limit any change they make so you continue to feel at home.

ATMOSPHERE

The layout of stores varies enormously, from the shop piled high with boxes and goods, to the simplicity of a cell phone store with low lighting and shiny steel. Whatever the decor, it is planned to create the best atmosphere to make you buy.

LIFESTYLE

If the store is selling a lifestyle product, it may have wider, more spacious aisles, cool colors, just a few carefully chosen items placed at eye level – even a seat or two – and music playing. It makes you feel special.

FAMILIARITY

We each have a few favorite stores where we like to buy things.

Displays offer lots of choices to hold your attention in the store.

We shop at the stores that have things we like.

An uncluttered window display can attract sophisticated buyers.

POP!

POP is shop speak for the point of purchase, sometimes called the point of sale – the place where you meet the product! In a store, this is the rack or shelf where the product is displayed. But is it all displayed at random on the off-chance that you might stop and pick it up? It's not!

Retailers knows that up to three quarters of all purchases are made by customers who are impulse-shopping around the store. They spend only ten seconds looking at any one rack or shelf. So the goods must all be displayed at the right level – within eyeshot and easy reach. They must be packaged to catch your eye.

But there must be entertainment as well! Free-standing displays mean you have to walk around or behind the product, perhaps look up or peep under. It's a game of hide-and-seek designed to keep you interested, to keep you guessing.

It's all done to make shopping fun!

BARGAINS

We all love a bargain. Nothing feels quite as good as buying something "cheap." Finding a bargain isn't difficult if you spend time hunting from store to store for the item that's a bit cheaper, or for the one marked down or on sale.

Street vendors often specialize in one kind of product.

THERE ARE PLENTY OF PLACES TO FIND THEM!

STREET VENDORS

Your town may have street vendors that stand on the street corner. They appear to sell the very same things as the stores – except they're far cheaper. But remember, if you want to return the product for any reason, the street vendor may not be there the next day. Street vendors can offer good deals and reasonable prices by selling clearance stock or stock from a company that has closed down.

BANKRUPT STOCK

Sales advertising merchandise liquidations are often genuine sales arising from the closure of a company. There will be good bargains to pick up, but remember to check that you still get a warranty, a guarantee that things will be fixed or exchanged if they go wrong.

BUYING ONLINE

Buying online should be cheaper. After all, there are no store costs to add to the price, no big buildings, no salespeople. But photos can make things look better than they are, colors don't match what you saw, or the fabric is a disappointment. However, you can return what you don't want. Remember to unwrap all products carefully – you'll need to repackage them exactly as they came if you want your money back in full. And always keep the receipt for returns.

OUTLET STORES

Outlet stores are a big part of the bargain-shopping scene. Designers and manufacturers of every kind of product change their designs and stock often. The old stuff must go to make way for the new. Outlet stores often specialize in designer labels and seasonal fashions.

THRIFT STORES

Thrift stores are full of bargains. They only sell the best of the stuff given to them. They have a big selection and you are doing some good when you buy. Most thrift stores are run to raise funds for a cause, so you're helping them in their efforts with every small purchase.

PRESSURE TO BUY

As you get older, there's increased pressure from all kinds of companies that want you to buy their stuff – and from some of your friends who've already got it! Manufacturers need to advertise to inform consumers about products. But it's also about persuading them to buy. It's about making you think you need something when maybe you don't.

PART OF THE CROWD

Advertisers think you're indecisive. They think you show no loyalty to any brand and will shift your spending to whatever is cool or most fashionable at the time. They use clever techniques, and almost all ads use one or more of them.
There's the ad that tells you if you don't buy you're going to feel left out, not "part of the crowd." Everyone else is right or knows something you don't.

But be an individual! Buy the things you want, however "different" and "strange" they may be. Recognize advertising for what it is ...

... AND MAKE YOUR OWN CHOICES!

PEER PRESSURE

There's nothing easy about resisting peer pressure. The need to fit in stays with us for most of our lives. Copying classmates and friends, aspiring to magazine pictures of the trendy, judging yourself by what others say about you, is all part of this pattern. You have to be pretty gutsy to stand out from the crowd and do your own thing.

BE YOURSELF!

Doing what is best for YOU, wearing what suits YOU, and expressing your own opinions, is part of being YOU and not a copycat of everybody else.

Remember that manufacturers, retailers, and advertisers worldwide are relying on you to do what everybody else does. They make money by creating mass fashions, mass attitudes, and mass buying fads.

Being one of the crowd is comfortable – but don't let your peers influence you too much.

GETTING TO YOU

Advertisers are spending billions of dollars a year to target your wallet, and you're watching thousands of their advertisements a year. That's a lot of pressure! The average young person will have received 250,000 media messages involving advertising by the time they're 15.

WHAT A WASTE!

How many pairs of jeans have you got in your closet? How many T-shirts, blouses, or other unworn clothes are there that have never been taken off the hanger? We buy for all kinds of reasons, but few are because we don't have something. It's more likely to be for a different reason – and not always one that makes a lot of sense.

SPOILED FOR CHOICE

If you want a chocolate bar, you have dozens to choose from. Need a breakfast cereal? There are dozens of those, too! A sweater – a hundred! A magazine? When it comes to food and clothing and entertainment, we're spoiled for choice.

WAY BACK WHEN ...

There was a time when things like these were not so readily available. In fact, during World War II, you had to take your ration book to the store to get your one permitted item. It was not that long ago! But today, with goods pouring in from all over the world, there's more than enough for everyone – and no one has to wait in line for a pair of winter boots.

SHOPAHOLICS!

Compared to the hard days of rationing, there's no doubt that we've become spoiled by the many choices. We can be wasteful, throwing things away because they're not new. We throw food away, not because it's spoiled, but because we have a crisper, fresher version. We throw a shirt away because it would cost more to take it to the dry cleaners than to replace it.

OVER-CONSUMING

In many developed countries, people have become such expert consumers that they overbuy knowingly. And many throw away a large proportion of what they buy and think nothing of it. The truth is, we've become very wasteful.

Waste often ends up in huge unsightly landfills like this one.

WHAT STATISTICS?

Statisticians record and evaluate data and create statistics about you and your spending habits.

Here are some interesting statistics:

Teens 'n tweens

Young teenagers – (13–15) are particularly savvy. They receive and spend more in an attempt to gain freedom from parents and from rules and routine. Life is focused on fun, fashion, and friends.

The many million strong group known as "tweens" – (8–12) have more spending power than ever before as working parents have extra income.

* Tweens want to feel and look older, like their older siblings, and their taste is for more grown-up products.
* They love cell phones.

A mobile world

Cell phones are a popular way to keep in touch with friends, play games, and find the latest apps.

* The world now has over 6.8 billion cell phones.
* The number of cell phones in use in the United States exceeds its population ... 327,000,000 phones!
* Over 69% of children have a cell phone by age 14.
* Text messaging is the top method of communicating for young people.

Advertising at you!

* Do you watch TV at certain times, in the early evening, and on Saturday mornings?
* Do you think there's too much advertising targeted at you?
* Do you think there's too much candy and fast-food advertising targeted at you?

WELL, YOU SHOULD!

This is because you spend so much! You make a real difference to the economy, so retailers and manufacturers want to know all about you!

Big spenders

Most of your spending money comes from pocket money or allowances. The rest comes from doing chores, from gifts, and from part-time jobs.

* But who spends most? Girls or boys?
* Who saves most? Girls or boys?

The answers are girls each time.

Pop Quiz

You see some expensive gym shoes. Do you:

* save until you can buy them?
* earn money from chores?
* pester a parent for the extra cash?
* ask for them as an advance birthday gift?

Your choice

Choose the things you most like to spend money on:

* movies/concerts
* clothes
* candy and snacks
* shoes
* computer games
* sporting events
* books
* cell phones
* magazines
* cosmetics and toiletries
* music
* other

Are you budgeting for all this?

WHAT CAN YOU LEARN FROM YOUR ANSWERS?

Give It Away!

There are many, many people on our planet who need help. If you watch television news reports, or even see appeals in newspapers, you must be aware of how difficult life is for people in poor countries or war-torn places. If you care about what goes on in the world and the people who share it with you – if you want to be a "citizen of the planet" and not a couch potato – then it's time to take an interest.

Refugees have fled from war or disasters at home. They live in makeshift homes until they can return.

Children receive food parcels from an overseas aid organization.

EVERY LITTLE BIT HELPS!

We all have needs and wants. Needs are things that we can't do without – things like food, water, clothing, and so on. Wants are things that we THINK we can't do without – things like ice cream, video games, and designer clothes. But of course we can do without some of these "wants" so we can help others. When you see pictures of refugees and the horror they're living through, it might be difficult to see what you can do to help.

But every little thing you can do or give really does help.

A GREAT FEELING

Giving to others less well off than yourself is not about going around feeling superior and smug. It's about knowing that someone out there will eat today because of what you've done.

And that has to make you feel like you've done something worthwhile.

HELPING ABROAD

We hear news every day of terrible poverty and hunger in overseas countries. You can shrug this off as someone else's problem – it's all too far away anyway. And why can't their governments help them?

But when a few people have a lot of money and most are begging for food, things certainly seem unbalanced. It IS possible to change things. We can each do a little, knowing that this will add up to a lot in the end.

THE HOMELESS

Many people, even in rich countries, are homeless. Contributing to charities that help the homeless takes them off the street and gives them shelter.

CHARITIES

A HELPING HAND

Charities are organizations that give help in many different forms to those in need. There are many well known charities you've heard of – and maybe helped from time to time.

Some charities can help people by rushing to a disaster zone and bringing immediate relief. Some work over the long term to improve education and health wherever they are based.

FOUNDATIONS

Foundations are also charities. These are set up by wealthy companies, individuals, or families to support certain projects with cash. Community foundations can be established to use specific funds for charitable purposes. They don't pay tax on their income, providing they give away a certain portion of their value each year to charity.

RAISING MONEY

Let's say there's a charity run planned. You have to run around your local park and some outlying woods in a sponsored event. For each mile that you run, various friends and family will sponsor you to the tune of $1 a mile. You could go as a group, as a whole family or your class at school could get involved. If there are another 50 people doing the same as you . . . that's big bucks!

How much you give is entirely up to you, of course. Settle on an amount you feel comfortable with, and remember that however small it is, by giving regularly, the donation starts to build into something really meaningful.

And don't forget that giving money is just one way of helping. You can give toys, books, and clothes to some charities – it all helps.

RICH AND POOR

Many people think that if they were richer, they'd be happier. Of course, people who have enough to be able to feed and clothe themselves and live a comfortable life are far happier than those who don't. But once you are comfortable, does having more money bring more happiness? Well, being rich doesn't guarantee happiness, and being rich isn't the ONLY way to be happy.

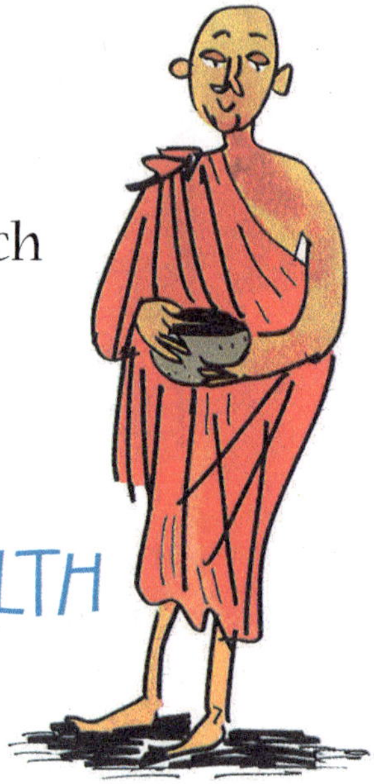

THE STRUGGLE FOR WEALTH

The great Indian leader Mohandas Gandhi believed that happiness came from living a simple life. He rejected wealth as a means to fulfillment, even to the point of sewing his own clothing.

People who think wealth and happiness go together can find themselves on an upward slope – always struggling to be richer and richer, and becoming more and more unhappy because they can't make it. In the end, they feel as if they've failed – they never quite made it to the top. However, feeling content with what you've achieved is almost certainly the key to happiness.

HAVING IT ALL

The amount of income a person earns helps decide how much they buy. If a person with a low income spends $5,000 on a trip around the world, they will have to cut back on buying food, clothing, or shelter. If a person with a high income makes the same investment, they may not need to cut back on anything.

PHILANTHROPY

The rich don't just spend on themselves. Many give millions away to charities or other causes they support. Such people are known as philanthropists. Philanthropy means helping others.

Borrowing

However hard you try to manage your budget, there are always going to be times when you need that extra bit. One of the key problems with running out of money when you really need it is that you have to ask someone to help. You have to find someone to lend you money and you have to borrow it on terms that are not too harsh.

FROM FRIENDS

Friends are more likely than anyone else to help you out with a loan – an interest-free loan! In other words, they'll lend you money to be repaid, dollar for dollar. Having said that, any loan is a debt. And debts have a nasty habit of turning sour.

While you owe money to a friend, you may get asked to help them out with favors and, of course, it's difficult to say "no."

Above all, remember that even if the loan is quite casual, it is a loan and not a gift. Friendships often fall apart when borrowers forget their obligations.

FROM PARENTS

Borrowing from parents can be as casual as borrowing from a friend – but not always. Depending on the amount of the loan, you'll need to negotiate how much and how often you make repayments.

And bear in mind there will be no further loans or helpful handouts if you get this wrong. They might tell you that you don't deserve a second chance, and they're right of course. If you've got the guts to borrow from them in the first place, you're certainly old enough to be taking responsibility for the repayments.

And parents might just charge interest – not necessarily in money terms, but they'll be bound to ask for those extra chores and help while you're in their debt.

DEBT AND CREDIT

It may seem odd to warn you about the dangers of debt when you're still just getting pocket money. But this isn't to advise you not to take on debt so much as to make you aware of the consequences of what may happen later on.

SEE IT COMING

Too often people are plunged into more debt because they just didn't realize how difficult things might become once they were in debt. It doesn't help when credit card companies and banks put us under pressure to borrow. So, if you're aware right now of what happens when you get into debt, you might just think twice about drifting down that route in the future.

CAN'T PAY

Debt doesn't become a problem until you're not able to pay it back. This is the part that needs to be avoided at all costs, even if it does mean doing without things you want.

When things get truly bad, there are people known as debt collectors who are employed to come to your home and take back all the things you now can't pay for ... just imagine!

The difficult stuff

A debt is what you owe to someone or to a company when you borrow money from them.

The trick with debt is to only borrow what you can afford to pay back over a set period of time. If you don't have enough money to cover the repayments each month, don't take the debt on. It seems simple, but many people get it wrong – and it's not always their fault. Any debt is a risk, so you need to cut the risk to a minimum.

What can being in debt mean?

The consequences of being in debt can be pretty grim:

* You worry about it all the time.
* You can't spend what you want.
* All your spare money goes into paying off the interest that's mounting on the debt.
* You can't see the end of it.

What is credit?

Credit is how much a lender decides can be loaned to you based on your financial value, or your net worth. The credit amount can be spent by you and must be repaid. If the lender has it right, this won't cause you too much hardship to repay. If they lend you too much, then problems could come up when trying to pay it back.

Budgeting

You are never too young to start a budget.

Budgeting is the simplest form of money management. It's not the most exciting part. In fact, spending, and even saving, beats budgeting by a long shot! But it's one of those things that gets easier (once you've done it).

Budgeting is like going to the dentist. It's a tough call, but you know it's doing you good!

CAN I AFFORD IT?

Making a budget means you recognize that your money supply is limited – and that's not fun! It almost certainly means that you want to do lots of things you know you may not be able to afford.

The good news is that once your budget is made up, it will stop you from worrying about whatever spending you're going to do, and that should make it all worthwhile!

YES I CAN!

A budget will almost certainly show you that there IS enough money to do the things you want. You may have to save over time to achieve them, even wait a little. You may have to buy something in parts rather than right away – your song collection, for example, or your new outfit!

NO I CAN'T

It's not always easy to put off doing something you want to do or buying something you think you need. We live in a world of promises. Get it now – pay later! Put it on a credit card! Worry about it when the bill turns up!

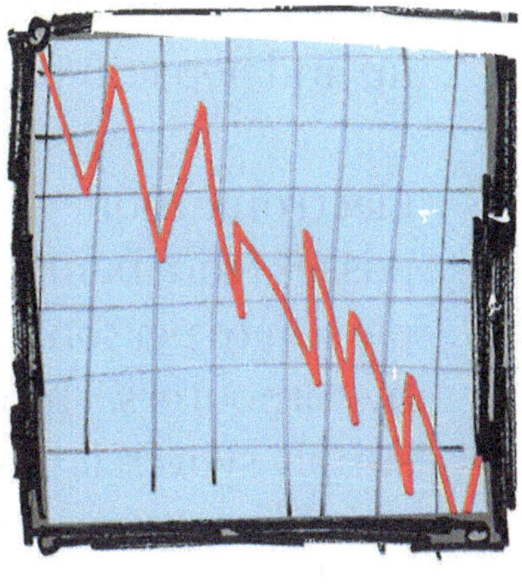

If you go along with this approach, you'll almost certainly suffer from bad budgeting habits. You may get someone to help you out because you're young or "you don't know any better" – but unfortunately, this will change. In the real world, the only people who'll help you out may want a lot of money to do so.

ABOVE ALL, BUDGETS REQUIRE SELF-DISCIPLINE.

What's Next for Money?

In the future, you may never have to use coins and paper money again. Instead, you'll use plastic cards such as credit or debit cards for all transactions. In other words, money will go electronic. Or it may go even further. It may "vanish" altogether!

So how can money be money when it doesn't look like money? In fact, when it doesn't look like anything because you can't even see it? You certainly can't pick it up and pop it in your pocket.

Electronic money is money that passes from bank to bank, person to person, all controlled by computers. The computers simply switch it from place to place using special codes.

AND THIS KIND OF MONEY DOESN'T HAVE TO BE REAL. IT CAN BE VIRTUAL.

REAL OR UNREAL?

This kind of money is called virtual currency or virtual money. "Virtual" describes something that doesn't physically exist so that you can see or touch it, but computer software makes it seem so. It's very close to actually being something without actually being it.

Does this sound like the kind of money you would trust? Probably not – but virtual money operates like real money, and more and more people are starting to use it. Just like traditional money, these currencies can be used to buy physical goods and services.

BITCOINS

One of these kinds of currency which became popular was the bitcoin. Bitcoins are electronically created and stored. Your piggy bank of bitcoins is in fact your computer. Bitcoins are exchanged using secret messaging for security so they can't be copied or stolen. And they don't belong to a bank or other institution so no one can interfere or control them.

Bitcoins and other forms of virtual money act as real money, and will have a place in our future.

FOR THE FUTURE ...

In your own lifetime, you might just see the end of those jingling coins and dollar bills. Technology is now learning to cope with the huge money transactions that speed around our planet on a minute-by-minute basis. There are likely to be more changes to the look and feel of money in the next 10 years than there ever have been!

AROUND AND AROUND

Today, huge amounts of money are shifted around the world in this way. Tomorrow, we may all deal in electronic money. You may accumulate THOUSANDS in your lifetime, but you'll never actually see a penny of it.

MONEY'S MONEY

All this probably won't affect you a great deal – unless you end up working in some kind of financial company. But you'll still have to earn money and pay the bills. The older you get, the more money will flow around and around you, bringing new responsibilities with it.

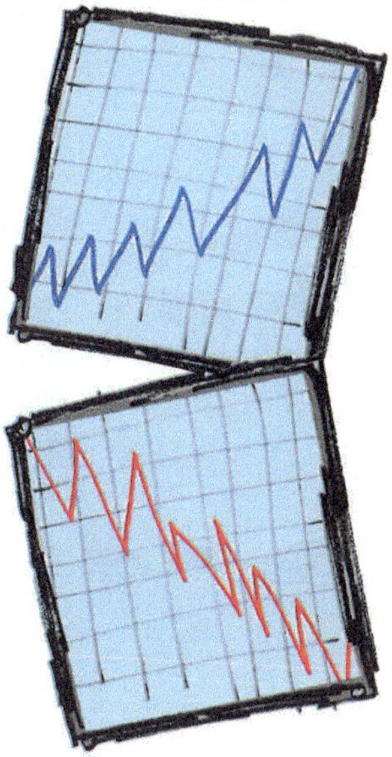

So the more you know about money, the better you'll be able to deal with it.

And the more you understand it...

... THE MORE CONTROL OVER YOUR MONEY YOU'LL HAVE.

Let's Discuss This!

How do you earn money?

If you're lucky, you'll be given an allowance to spend as you like. What chores could you do that would help your family? You can also ask neighbors or family friends if they will pay you to do some small jobs.

What's wrong with shopping?

Nothing at all if you really need to buy something. But DON'T shop for entertainment! The best way to shop is to write a list of what you will buy while shopping – and stick to it. Think of some other ways you can control your spending.

Why do you need a bank?

If you put a little money in a savings account each week or month, the bank rewards you by paying you interest. Discuss how you can open a bank account with your parents and what you'd like to buy with your savings.

Why do you need to budget?

You will soon discover that money doesn't stretch, giving you everything you want. Why not create a wish list with the price of each item so you know how much you need to save in your account? You could even give yourself a deadline to earn and save the money before a certain date.

Additional Resources

BOOKS

Donovan, Sandra. *Thrift Shopping: Discovering Bargains and Hidden Treasures.* Minneapolis, Minnesota: Twenty-First Century Books, 2015.

Kemper, Bitsy. *Budgeting, Spending, and Saving.* Minneapolis, Minnesota: Lerner Publishing Group, 2015.

Larson, Jennifer. *Do I Need It or Do I Want It?* Minneapolis, Minnesota: Lerner Publishing Group, 2010.

Glossary

allowance
(see pocket money)

bank account
A person's agreement with a bank to hold onto their money.

bitcoin
An experimental currency which exists only in computer and Internet buying and selling.

budget
An agreed sum to be spent.

charity
An organization that gives help in many different forms to those in need.

consumer
A person who buys products on a regular basis and whose buying habits can be predicted.

credit
Amount of money that can be borrowed.

credit card
A card that lets you use borrowed money to buy goods.

currency
A form of money in notes and coins that is used for buying and selling.

debit
An amount taken out of a bank account as a payment.

debt
Borrowed money to be repaid.

depreciate
The value of something that decreases over time.

donation
A gift of money, usually to a charity.

electronic money
Money that is not "real" but which exists only in the world of Internet and computers.

income
Money that is earned by working.

interest
A percentage sum added to borrowed or invested money.

loan
An amount of money that is given to someone, but which must be paid back.

money cycle
Another term to describe how money moves around and around as it is used to buy and sell goods.

net worth
The total value of someone's personal money and valuable goods.

peer pressure
The phrase used to describe how people of the same age can influence each other to do things.

pester power
A phrase to describe how children can influence their parents to buy them things.

pocket money
Money paid to a child for their personal spending.

point of purchase
A special place in a store where goods are displayed in an eye-catching way.

prices
The cost of buying certain items.

profit
The money that is made by a seller which is more than the actual cost of the goods.

spending power
A term used to describe the money available to spend of a particular group of people.

statistics
Mathematical figures that can be used to count how people behave.

virtual money
Money that exists in computer form only, but which has an accepted value just like real money.

warranty
A guarantee that is issued by a seller when they sell products and which promises the products are in good condition and will be repaired if they are faulty.

Index